# BIG DATA

How to get value from data with Business Intelligence &

Marketing Technologies in Management 4.0

**TOMMASO MAZZIOTTI**

TOMMASO MAZZIOTTI

TOMMASO MAZZIOTTI

# TABLE OF CONTENTS

TOMMASO MAZZIOTTI

# Introduction

Big data refers to a large quantity of structured and unstructured data. This is used when traditional methods for extracting value from data sets becomes futile. When the data sets become too big to analyze, more advanced and sophisticated tools, systems, and techniques need to be on-boarded to make use of this data. While many believe too much data can harm their system, in fact, the more data is collected, the more insight you can gain. Big data is distinguished by:

- Velocity

- Variety

- Volume

- Value

- Veracity

It is not just the amount of data that is considered. Big data also includes many different types of data that flow in at an incredibly fast rate, which is readily available in real-time. The data also must be of value, which means it must contain information allowing for new insight to be discovered or to be used in ways never possible before.

For businesses, this is especially vital because advanced technology is making it easier than ever to access this wide variety of data to drive their businesses forward. Businesses are beginning to realize that it isn't enough to just gather more data—they need to be able to understand what this data means. With such a high volume, however, many companies are not taking full advantage of all they can uncover and the insight they can gain from this big data that can significantly impact the growth of their operations.

Unfortunately, data is collected and stored, and little is ever done with it because all that can be done is not fully understood. Big data was the key motivator behind data science, as the approaches used in data science revolve around deciphering large amounts of data. But companies have had always collected and stored data and have a massive amount of data stored in databases. Big data and databases are two different entities— while many companies can have large databases, they can also obtain big data.

## How does big data differ from the database?

It is understandable how databases and big data can be confused, as they seem to refer to the same things. Both involve large amounts of data, but there is a major difference between the two. Big data encompasses all types and forms of data. Databases, on the other hand, refers to where data is stored. Databases can be used to store big data, but that does not mean the database itself is considered big data. Databases are simply the structures used to store data. Big data could be what is being stored. While they may seem to be similar, databases and big data are two different elements of data science.

You can have a lot of data stored in databases, but big data tends to refer more toward the amount of data that flows in from multiple sources over a concise amount of time, as opposed to databases, which store a lot of data sets which have been collected over a specific period of time.

## Data Defined

Data can come in a variety of forms and can be obtained from multiple sources. What is considered data can range from colors present in an image to the age of a new customer. Informations collected from a website in terms of views, visits, and navigation are also some forms of data. This can be visual, numerical, text, models, variables, videos, and sounds, or any set of characters.

Because data can come in such diverse forms, it needs to be organized systematically. Data is organized by data sets. A data set consists of specific variables and lists the values associated with these variables. Data sets can also include files or documents and can be formulated by algorithms, which can be used for software testing. Data types have an impact on the variables you discover, as well as the tools you use to analyze it.

CHAPTER 1:

# Introduction: Welcome to a Smarter World

About 90% of all data in recorded human history has only been generated in the last decade. But the need to use and understand data has been around for centuries, even millennia. As a matter of fact, Mesopotamians have been discovered to use early forms of accounting to keep track of their herds and crops.

The use of accounting has gradually improved, and in the 1600s, Great Britain used a far more complex system to record and examine all information about mortality rolls in London. The early statistician John Graunt wanted to understand and build a sophisticated warning system for the Black Death that ravaged Europe.

Graunt recorded the first example of statistical data analysis where he archived his discoveries in his book Natural and Political Observations Made upon the Bills of Mortality. Graunt is regarded nowadays as the father of statistics, because of this great work.

Throughout the 1800s, Information Age flourished in Europe and in the Americas. In 1887, modern data was first gathered by Herman Hollerith who invented the computing machine that is capable of interpreting holes punched into the paper cards to organize data for a census.

In the time of US President Franklin Delano Roosevelt, the country pioneered a significant data project to monitor the social security contributions of employees across the US. The US government commissioned IBM to develop a machine for the significant task.

During World War II, the United Kingdom developed the first data processing machine designed to decipher codes intercepted from the Nazis. The device was called Colossus, which had the capacity to search for patterns in codes at 5000 characters p/s.

It was a breakthrough invention as it significantly reduced the time needed to complete the task - from weeks, even months, to merely hours and even minutes.

The United States National Security Agency was created in 1952, and after only a decade, it has secured contracts with around 12000 cryptologists. The agency was tasked with the monumental undertaking of interpreting information during the Cold War as they began automatically gathering and decoding intelligence reports.

In 1965, the American Government funded the project to create several data centers to archive 172 million sets of fingerprints and 742 million tax returns. The task required data specialists to transfer all files into magnetic computer tape and keep them in one file location.

However, the project was discontinued over privacy protests from the public, but it signified the start of the era of the digital data storage.

Tim Berners Lee, a British computer scientist, invented a network of data sharing system, which was eventually known as the World Wide Web.

The system was designed to host share information through the hypertext. This invention paved the way for changing how the world consumes data.

Starting in the 1990s, millions of data were generated at an unprecedented rate as more and more people need to be connected to the web. The first supercomputer was developed in 1995. The computer has the capacity to perform calculations in a second compared to an ordinary calculator used by one person could in 30,000 years.

## The Era of Big Data

The term Big Data was coined by Roger Mougalas of O'Reilly Media, which was the company that coined the term Web 2.0. Mougalas used this term to refer to a dataset that can be impossible to organize and process using conventional tools for business intelligence.

At the same time, Google created MapReduce on top of Yahoo's Hadoop, which both aimed to index the whole web. At present, many organizations around the world are using the open-source platform of Hadoop to interpret large data sets.

As more platforms appeared including social networking sites, the rate of data creation increased rapidly. Soon, startups started mining this vast amount of data and governments also started funding data projects. In fact, in 2009, India funded a massive data project to store all fingerprints, pictures, and iris scan of its 1.2 billion citizens. This massive data is stored in the largest biometric database in the globe.

According to a 2-11 report published by McKinsey entitled Big Data: The Next Frontier for Innovation, Competition, and Productivity, by 2018, the US will need around 200,000 data scientists and about 1.5 million data managers. Hence, the role of Big Data Scientist is regarded as the most in-demand job today.

As a response, more and more Big Data startups appear to help organizations manage and make sense of big data. As businesses are now gradually adopting Big Data, similar to its welcome gesture in 1993 for the Internet, the revolution for Big Data is still ahead of us. Hence, we are expecting to see a lot of changes.

As a matter of fact, the volume of data is growing fast at such an unprecedented rate that we just can't use the old decimal point system. Nowadays, US agencies like the FBI and NSA are now using yottabytes, in computing their data volumes.

Basically, new terms are being coined to refer to the volume of data that is projected to be generated in the future.

Societies and organizations around the world will be completely changed by Big Data. Data scientists project that the volume of data that is currently available will be doubled every two years.

# CHAPTER 2:

# Smarter Business

B asically, anything that is digital is considered as data. Today, current software and hardware cannot handle the vast volume of various forms of data being generated at such an unprecedented pace.

Big Data has become too dynamic and sophisticated for conventional tools that we have today. It requires complex tools for effective processing, storage, analysis, and management. The volume of data that we are facing is so vast that our software and hardware technologies are lagging behind to keep up.

However, data scientists also developed tools and technologies to make sense of Big Data, so they can be used for specific purposes. The insights gained from this information could be used to aid business decisions, enhance efficiency, increase sales, and decrease costs. Big Data has become a significant element in modern business, and it has changed the landscape across industries.

Today, many companies spend a lot of time and money on the collection and analysis of data, but why are they doing this? And what are they benefiting from it?

Data is basically all of the information collected by a business each day. For this data to be collected, each sale must be recorded, but individual sales are not going to provide the company with much information.

However, when looked at in large groups, this data can provide companies with a ton of information. It can allow them to understand sales trends, what is making the most profit, what days of the week provide the most sales, as well as what is not selling and what days they are making the lowest profit.

Information like this can be vital when it comes to running a business. Let's say, for example, you are running a bakery and after analyzing the data, you have found that the majority of cakes are ordered on Friday, but no cakes are ordered on Monday. This will allow you to ensure you have plenty of cakes available on Friday when you know they will sell and only one or two available on Monday to reduce your losses for the day.

On top of this, by using this data, you will be able to decide if you want to run a promotion on Mondays to boost your sales on that day each week. You may also be able to cut back on the number of employees you need each Monday, because sales are so low, which will, of course, save you money in the long run.

Big Data has become extremely important for businesses because we live in a world that is constantly changing. This means that businesses are constantly changing as well. Because so many changes are taking place, businesses have to be able to keep up with these changes. You see, a business that is always struggling to catch up is not going to be a successful business.

You will also be able to use Big Data to ensure that you have satisfied customers and if you find that your customers are unhappy, you will be able to make the changes necessary to keep them coming back.

In the past, most data were used by the IT team of a company, which meant that any changes that needed to take place or anything that needed to be addressed were done so behind the scenes. This often meant that a company would submit a request for a change and the IT team would handle it. Today, however, most companies want to analyze the data for themselves, and they want to have access to all of the information.

The types of data that businesses collect can be vast and it really depends on the type of data that is generated by the company's specific product.

This type of data is going to allow you to see where you need to improve when it comes to sales, what specific products your customers are interested in, and what products they are not interested in at all. This will also help you to ensure that you are actually earning money each day instead of losing it.

Another type of data that is collected is qualitative data. This type of data is collected directly from the customers, usually via a survey. I'm sure that you have looked at a receipt at some point and noticed the little survey website listed at the bottom. Often times, this will state that there is some type of reward that can be won if the survey is filled out.

Why would companies do this? This is done so that companies can get more than just numerical data, so they can get real data from the customers who come into their business. Some companies may ask about the cleanliness of the business, if items were stocked on the shelves, if items were easy to find, and if the customer was happy with the overall experience.

Of course, not everyone is going to fill out this survey, but when a company gets 100 surveys filled out, and when analyzing the data finds out that 84% of the customers said that the product they were looking for was not in stock, the company now knows there is a problem with stocking or that they need to have more product on hand to satisfy their customers.

As I stated, the types of data that can be gathered are endless as are the ways that the data can be collected. This often leads companies into a trap because they feel that the more data they have, the better off the company will be.

Most data managers are spending at least two hours of their working day searching for data; however, what they are finding is that about 80% of the data they have to work with is completely useless.

This means that when data collection is taking place, companies need to be more careful about what data they are collecting. To ensure that data that is not useful is not being collected, it is important for the company to first determine what data is important to them and their company.

For example, let's say that your business is selling products on a website. Before each customer orders a product, they are asked to fill out specific questions. Although it would be great for a company selling weight loss products to know the average weight of their first time customers, it would not be important for a company selling perfume, for example.

This is where many companies become confused because after they have collected as much data as possible, they are left to sift through it and try to figure out what it means for them as a company.

To determine what information should be collected, a company should look at the top three challenges they are currently facing. The next step is to ask who should be involved in the process. Then ask if there are already many systems in place that could collect the data. Finally, you need to determine how the data will be tracked.

One of the biggest issues with data gathering is that many companies are unable to justify the cost or identify any return on their investment. If you cannot determine a return on the investment, then chances are, that bit of data does not matter.

However, if you can justify the cost by knowing that the information you are going to gather is going to help you increase sales or improve customer relations, then that is the type of data you want to gather.

To put all of this together, you want to start small. Focus on the areas of your business that you know need the most improvement. As you improve upon your data collection in those areas, you will be able to branch out into other areas, ensuring that you are collecting the right data for your business.

By looking at the data collected, most of the time, companies are going to find that everything is fine, but there is always going to be that one anomaly that is going to tell them there is something that can be improved upon. It is finding those anomalies that is important if a company wants the data to help them increase sales.

However, there are going to be times when a company finds that the data they are collecting is showing them that everything is, in fact, not okay and that is when the data collection is the most important because it could be what actually saves the business from going under.

By looking at the data and understanding what changes need to be made, a company can actually turn things around. However, if that company did not gather that data or never paid attention to what the data was telling them, chances are, they would not be a business much longer.

CHAPTER 3:

# Start with Strategy

A big data strategy is going to involve the collection, storage, retrieval, analysis, and actionable insights. The goal of a big data strategy is to build a big data foundation that can power business intelligence.

The collection is not an issue for most businesses, but many businesses err by pre-judging the value of data that they could collect, thus not collecting as much data as they should. By now, you should recognize that data may have insights that are not readily apparent. This is the benefit of machine learning and the role that it plays in data analysis: finding hidden patterns that humans didn't know existed and - frankly – couldn't have known existed. Therefore, you need to collect data with an open mind. Any bit of information that a business can collect is potentially useful.

The second issue that needs to be addressed as part of a big data strategy is the storage and retrieval of the data. A large amount of infrastructure is needed to handle the volume and velocity of big data. This includes large storage capacity as well as powerful computers. It is difficult for organizations, especially smaller to mid-sized businesses, to build the kind of data-driven infrastructure that will enable them to handle big data effectively. Doing so could literally require hundreds of computer servers with huge banks of data storage and highly efficient data retrieval tools. In addition, a high level of cybersecurity is necessary to protect the integrity of the data.

For many businesses, these requirements mean that they are going outside the organization to have these needs met. Cloud computing has made this possible, and many of the world's largest companies are offering accessible cloud computing resources that are cost-effective, fast, and easily used to store and retrieve data on a 24/7 basis. Providers of such services include Amazon, Microsoft, and Google. These companies offer several levels of cloud services that can be tailored to fit the needs of any business size, from a one-person operation running as a home business up to a large corporation, or even a government entity. For example, Amazon's Simple Storage Service, known as Amazon S3, can be used by businesses of any size for low-cost cloud computing services.

Companies that can deploy their own big data systems can utilize open source tools to get the job done. This includes using Apache tools such as Hadoop and Spark, along with MapReduce. Careful considerations must be made. Handling the job internally will keep the data under the direct control of the company. However, this will entail having to build out or rent massive computer storage capacity that must be maintained on a 24/7 basis. That will also require a robust set of information security measures to ensure the integrity of the data and protect it from hacking, corruption, and other problems. This will also require hiring a large amount of staffing.

Even though many larger businesses might have the capacity to implement their own completely internal big data strategy, it's not clear that doing, so is always the best way forward. This decision will have to be made by each organization. However, the fact that established companies like Microsoft and IBM are available for providing infrastructure and services that are already thoroughly tested and robust makes outsourcing these tasks a viable and more cost-effective option.

By utilizing third-party services, you can massively reduce the cost of implementing a big data strategy. Big data capabilities will be provided for you by established companies that have already developed massive computer infrastructure for storing, maintaining, and securing data. Third-party sources like IBM, Google, and Microsoft may also be able to assist with analytics.

Once the collection, storage, and retrieval problems are solved, systems must be put in place to make sense of the data. By itself, the data is useless. To be used for the kind of data-driven decision making that business intelligence entails, the patterns, relationships, and trends in the data must be discovered and put in a presentable form for human analysis. These steps will involve the use of data science and machine learning. This is another step where a company will have to decide whether it wants to do this internally or outsource the task.

There are several arguments that can be made for outsourcing the task for small and mid-sized businesses. Many companies like IBM have a long history of developing artificial intelligence and machine learning tools, and they are making their capabilities available as business services they are providing for clients at an effective cost. BM has been a leader in this area since artificial intelligence first became a field, so you know you are getting high levels of reliability. This is not a recommendation for or against IBM, but rather to let you know that these types of services are available. They are also available from other large companies like Microsoft, Facebook, and Google, as well as from many newer and startup companies.

Many large corporations are doing this internally, Southwest Airlines is one example.

Either way, a part of your big data strategy is going to include developing a data science team. If you outsource your big data analysis, you may still need an internal data scientist to collaborate with third-party teams to get the most out of the data. Data scientists can be hired internally, or you can work with contract providers.

Machine learning tools for doing data analysis is also available for internal use, and you can hire data scientists to develop their own tools. Depending on your specific needs, there may be off-the-shelf software tools that you can use, and they are already proven to be reliable and effective. For this reason, you may not necessarily want to hire a team of data scientists to develop your own internal tools. Of course, if the expense can be managed and there are special needs in a company that cannot be addressed by off-the-shelf components, this can be an option to pursue as a part of your big data strategy. Another alternative is to utilize existing services from companies like IBM, Google, and

Microsoft to turn your big data into insights that can be incorporated into business intelligence.

The final part of a big data strategy is engaging in data-driven decision making based on the actionable insights that have been derived from this process. This is going to become a central part of the business process, operation, and organization. This is because it is a continuous process. Machine learning is not a one-time event; it is going on constantly as large volumes of data continue to be collected. It operates in this way to be able to provide new insights often on a real-time basis after the infrastructure has been established.

In each case, the actionable insights provided by this process are going to provide a basis for business intelligence as well as provide inputs for business intelligence. Human insight and ingenuity will be brought to bear in many cases. Not every insight is going to have an equal value to the enterprise. Therefore, all the existing components of business intelligence will have to be applied in order to determine which actions can and should be taken by the organization. Issues such as cost-effectiveness are going to be central, as well as the ability of the company to carry out each action from a practical standpoint. The allocation of limited resources to different possible actions is another factor. The leaders of the business at all levels of management will have to weigh each possible action against others. This is nothing new, and businesses may have to forgo some actionable insights even if they are valuable in favor of others that are going to be impactful and be more cost-effective. The situation will have to be evaluated and re-evaluated on a consistent basis as more data continues to come in.

Not all possible actions that come out of the application of machine learning and AI to big data are going to require the input of humans. In many cases, these systems will be operating autonomously and without human input, other than a periodic review. Examples of these types of applications include cybersecurity and fraud detection in financial matters.

Many people new to the concept of machine learning are hesitant even put off - by the autonomous capabilities that it offers. However, this can be a huge competitive advantage for the organization. Rather than making humans useless, it frees them up so they can be used for higher-level and more important tasks. It also helps the company work far more efficiently, both internally and externally. An example of this is frontline customer support operations. By using an AI system to handle this, employees can be dedicated to handle customer problems that are of a more serious and impactful nature. This will improve the ability of the company to respond to customer complaints and problems by providing better service. However, one side-effect of this: companies and society at large will have to devote more resources to employee training so that they are able to perform at a higher level that requires a larger and more sophisticated job skillset.

CHAPTER 4:

# Apply Analytics

T he terms of big data and big data analytics are often used interchangeably, going to the fact that the inherent purpose of big data is to be analyzed. "Big data analytics" can be defined as a set of qualitative and quantitative methods that can be employed to examine a large amount of unstructured, structured and semi-structured data to discover data patterns and valuable hidden insights. Big data analytics is the science of analyzing big data to collect metrics, key performance indicators and Data trends that can be easily lost in the flood of raw data, buy using machine learning algorithms and automated analytical techniques. The different steps involved in "big data analysis" are:

Gathering Data Requirements: It is important to understand what information or data needs to be gathered to meet the business objective and goals. Data organization is also very critical for efficient and accurate data analysis. Some of the categories in which the data can be organized are gender, age, demographics, location, ethnicity, and income. A decision must also be made on the required data types (qualitative and quantitative) and data values (can be numerical or alphanumerical) to be used for the analysis.

Gathering Data: Raw data can be collected from disparate sources such as social media platforms, computers, cameras, other software applications, company websites, and even third-party data providers. The big data analysis inherently requires large volumes of data, the majority of which is unstructured with a limited amount of structured and semi-structured data.

Data organization and categorization: Depending on the company's infrastructure, Data organization could be done on a simple Excel spreadsheet or using and man tools and applications that are capable of processing statistical data. Data must be organized and categorized based on data requirements collected in step one of the big data analysis process.

Cleaning the data: To perform the big data analysis sufficiently and rapidly, it is very important to make sure the data set is void of any redundancy and errors. Only a complete data set fulfilling the Data requirements must proceed to the final analysis step. Preprocessing of data is required to make sure the only high-quality data is being analyzed, and company resources are being put to good use.

Analyzing the data: Depending on the insight that is expected to be achieved by the completion of the analysis, any of the following four different types of big data analytics approach can be adopted:

Predictive analysis: This type of analysis is done to generate forecasts and predictions for future plans of the company. By the completion of predictive analysis on the company's big data, the future state of the company can be more precisely predicted and derived from the current state of the company. The business executives are keenly interested in this analysis to make sure the day-to-day company operations are in line with the future vision of the company. For example, to deploy advanced analytical tools and applications in the sales division of a company, the first step is to analyze the leading source of data. Once believes source analysis has been completed, the type and number of communication channels for the sales team must be analyzed. This is followed by the use of machine learning algorithms on customer data to gain insight into how the existing customer base is interacting with the company's products or services. This predictive analysis will conclude with the deployment of artificial intelligence-based tools to skyrocket the company's sales.

Prescriptive analysis: Analysis that is carried out by primarily focusing on the business rules and recommendations to generate a selective analytical path as prescribed by the industry standards to boost company performance. The goal of this analysis is to understand the intricacies of various departments of the organization and what measures should be taken by the company to be able to gain insights from its customer data by using the prescribed analytical pathway. This allows the company to embrace domain specificity and conciseness by providing a sharp focus on its existing and future big data analytics process.

Descriptive analysis: All the incoming data received and stored by the company can be analyzed to produce insightful descriptions on the basis of the results obtained. The goal of this analysis is to identify data patterns and current market trends that can be adopted by the company to grow its business. For example, credit card companies often require risk assessment results on all prospective customers, to be able to make predictions on the likelihood of the customer failing to make their credit payments and make a decision whether the customer should be approved for the credit or not. This risk assessment it's primarily based on the customer's credit history but also takes into account other influencing factors, including remarks from other financial institutions that the customer had approached for credit, customer income and financial performance as well as their digital footprint and social media profile.

Diagnostic analysis: As the name suggests, this type of analysis is done to "diagnose" or understand why a certain event unfolded and how that event can be prevented from occurring in the future or replicated if needed. For example, web marketing strategies and campaigns often employ social media platforms to get publicity and increase their goodwill. Not all campaigns are as successful as expected; therefore, learning from failed campaigns is just as important, if not more. Companies can run diagnostic analysis on their campaign by collecting data pertaining to the "social media mentions" of the campaign, number of campaign page views, the average amount of time spent on the campaign page by an individual, number of social media fans and followers of the campaign, online reviews and other related metrics to understand why the campaign failed and how future campaigns can be made more effective.

The big data analysis can be conducted using one or more of the tools listed below:

Hadoop – Open source data framework.

Python – Programming language widely used for machine learning.

SAS – Advanced analytical tool used primarily for big data analysis.

Tableau – Artificial intelligence-based tool used primarily for data visualization.

SQL – Programming language used to extract data from relational databases.

Splunk – Analytical tool used to categorize machine-generated data

R-programming – the Programming language used primarily for statistical computing.

CHAPTER 5:

# A Step-By-Step Guide for Conducting Data Analysis for Your Business

## Organizing Your Existing Data

The first step to utilizing data is to organize and categorize the data that you have. This necessary step is used so that software can analyze the data to find trends and correlations as well as solve various optimization problems. The categorization of data is also necessary for determining the additional data that your business may need to collect. Where this data has been stored will be vastly different depending on the business and the number of electric records that it keeps. Some basic records that all businesses have are employee salaries, employee health care costs, overhead costs broken down by category (electric, rcnt, etc.), total sales broken down into the smallest time scale that can easily be done, products sold with profit margins on each product, transactions done by cash and credit card and a few others that will be specific to your business.

The organization of data, and the accurate reporting of it, is extremely important for producing accurate results for every analytical statistic that you will look at. As you organize your data and create categories, mark the data that comes from electronic records. This will signify data that is absolutely accurate. To record this data, either use Microsoft Excel or a similar program. For free software, Google Sheets offers a great software package that can save results in multiple formats.

Take your time with this first step, as I understand the arduous and repetitive nature of data entry for your small businesses. Believe me when I say that, it becomes much easier when you have some existing data sets to work with. We want to have a decent number of categories for our data, because while you may know some of the problems you wish to solve, other problems in the future will use this data; you just don't know it yet.

Most of the data you enter will be recorded by the month, such as your utility bills and rent, as well as healthcare costs. The time measurement for salary is determined if your employees are paid by the hour, or on a yearly salary. You will want to input this data as one unit, meaning the dollar figure per time unit you decided with your employee. In the United States, 99% of the time, this is either hourly or yearly. The most important small unit time increment is in revenue generated; however, based on the firm, there are some exceptions. For most businesses, you will want revenue per hour; this is especially true with firms that operate with a customer facing storefront. You will want the smallest time unit because many optimization problems are often solved on a per-hour unit of measurement, and revenue per hour can always be extrapolated to larger time scales. If your firm seeks revenue through contracted projects, or client accounts, recording your revenue is done slightly different.

# Tools for Data Visualization

There are many different tools for visualizing your data, ranging in cost and purpose. This is a list of some of the most popular software tools and their common feature sets. For more information about visualizing data, as well as a statistic that should be used by more businesses.

**SAS**: Software & Solutions, this company offers a diverse range of tools for visualizing your existing data, ultimately helping you to better understand the main profit drivers in your business. Their service includes optimization tools that are mainly built towards businesses selling individual products, and not contractual work. This is one of the most costly toolsets on this list, but their services are very in-depth. The cost of SAS might be worth it for their customer service; however, their forums are useful even if you do not use their software. Their customer base is large and the type of businesses they attract are diverse. You will find useful information on their forums because the questions asked can be applied to nearly all statistical software.

**Fusion Charts**: For pure visualization of data, 'Fusion Charts' is probably your best bet on this list. The software itself is easy to use, and you can visualize your data before you pay for the full product. The trial software allows you to enter your data and use a handful of charts and graphs in a limited capacity. If you are a contractor and want to sort through the data you've accumulated, this is a good bet. For a small business, especially one that sells a number of products, 'Fusion Charts' is harder to recommend. There is one exception though; the tools are really great for presenting data to investors.

**Google Charts**: Free software for visualizing your data, I like to think about this as Fusion Charts lite. It will get the job done, but it won't be as engaging. There are a few advantages here that none of the other software packages have, mostly coming from the ever expanding nature of Google's API. While Google is well known for dropping support of several of its products, 'Google Charts' has been going strong for a number of years.

**Clear Story Data**: If cost is not an issue, Clear Story is probably going to fit your needs. The advantage of their software package is the pool of data that is already stored within their suite. They have data from many different businesses, recorded anonymously, or through existing government data. This data can be used to solve optimization problems even if you yourself don't have every necessary piece of information.

Businesses Specific Analytics And Managing Tools: For your business sector, there are specific tools that you can purchase to aid you in a variety of different ways beyond visualization, projections and optimizations. The software available covers common businesses such as grocery stores, pharmacies and gas stations, as well as landlords and more. Each industry will have a few different packages available, and depending on what you want to accomplish, this could be your best bet.

## Social Media Analytics

It's likely that your business has some form of social media presence, whether through Twitter or Facebook. You may try and promote sales on these sites, use them for customer feedback, or simply have a page to cross off that box on a checklist. All of these are totally valid reasons for creating your social media page. Truly, how you use social media doesn't matter as much right now as to how you can use social media to get a demonstration of simple analytics for your business. Using Google Analytics, you can get a sense of just some of the useful metrics that analytics can provide. Google Analytics is free to use (a small business should not pay for Google Analytics Premium) and offers a variety of measuring tools and stored data. A lot of this data will not increase your sales, and it might be hard to run optimizations on what Google provides, but I suggest you tinker on Google's webpage and take a look at peak traffic times to your social media page, how many unique users you get and peak times on larger scales like seasons or years. You can gleam some useful information such as growth in your online presence, or the number of attempts by hackers to take over your page, something every webpage must deal with.

## How to Conduct Data Analysis to Enhance Your Businesses

At this point, you should have already organized several data sets based on information already collected at your business. The next step is to decide on whether you want to solve a complex optimization problem such as the optimal opening and closing times of your business, or a simpler visual analysis of where your revenue is coming from. Visualization tools will provide you with new insight into your operating costs and where your revenue comes from, while optimization tools will provide theoretical answers to the problems you pose. This brings us to a very important part of business analytics. At the end of the day, analytics in business is hypothesis testing. This means that for whatever decision you make, whether it is where a product is placed on a shelf or the hours of your store, you must compare it to a second data set where that variable is different. Changing your store hours is a serious change, as you don't want to confuse your existing customer base; however, you will need to compare your revenue and operating costs to when your store hours were different. You cannot take it at faith value that any software package will always provide the best result. Optimizations in business will always require testing. For the use of visualization tools, these are also best used for hypothesis testing. A common outcome of using visualization tools is attempting to promote items that have a higher profit margin, typically by up selling to a consumer or placing those products where customers are more likely to see them. The visualization tools have to be returned to after some time has passed to verify that the changes to your business have indeed increased revenue. Optimization is a process of small tweaks that lead to the best outcomes. We have already covered several examples of small businesses of all sorts benefitting from data analytics to solve optimization problems and increase customer happiness.

## Sustainable Success Through Data

Your willingness to test new business ideas and compare them to how you operated your firm is the key to your success. The changes you make to your business are most useful when you gain data to back up or refute their usefulness. Make sure that as you adapt your business and solve for optimization problems, or if you are trying new products and services, that you are comparing the changes you have made to a proper time scale. Changes that you make that might negatively affect your bottom line should be followed through with enough time to verify that the effects are negative. Kroger supermarkets were taken as an example of hypothesis testing and analytics done right. There were entire financial quarters where they suffered because of experimentation, but it needed to be done to verify the results. When you make changes to your business, you must account for both the possible positive or negative effects. Do not attempt to make changes to your business or how it operates unless you are willing to endure potential negative effects; it is businesses that understand this, that use hypothesis testing and analytics to their strongest effect.

## Risk Management Tips

Optimizing one's business and increasing revenue comes with inherent risk. You may alienate customers as your business changes to take on new challenges. You may have information problems with your customers as hours, staff or price change in your business. This is the major risk of business optimization, and firms of all sizes must come to deal with this major issue. There are a couple of ways to mitigate the risk of losing customers as you adapt your business for increased profits; you must have clear messaging to your existing customer base and you must focus on small optimizations and not full on business overhauls.

**CHAPTER 6:**

# The Data Science Process

T he data science process involves solving problems related to data science. There is a framework of data science that is followed during the project life cycle. Certain key skills and requirements are present in the complete project life cycle of data science. Data scientists analyze enormous sets of seemingly dissimilar data to reveal astonishing insights in the field. The procedure they use is a secret to most individuals outside the circle of data science. The following are the detailed steps required to solve a particular problem in the scenario of data science:

## • Consider The Problem

The first action a data scientist takes before solving a problem is to describe precisely what the problem is. Data scientists have to be able to decipher data queries into something over which action can be taken. A data scientist will get vague responses from individuals who have certain issues. A data scientist will have to get the instinct to change rare responses into actionable results.

## • Gather The Data

The second stage of data science development is very simple. In this step, the data scientists gather the data that they require for data science from obtainable data sources. During this step, the data scientists must query the databases by consuming their practical skills such as MySQL to gather the data. Data experts will obtain data in file arrangements such as Microsoft Excel etc. If the data experts are utilizing programming languages like R or Python, they will have access to precise packages that can read statistics from these data sources right into the data science algorithms and programs. Data experts gather data from databases as well as by connecting to web APIs. The most basic way of getting information is directly from the files. Some websites allow the use of their Web APIs to gather their data.

For the tasks mentioned above, a data expert will need particular expertise. This expertise will include the management of databases. To get big data groups, a data scientist will use distributed storage such as Spark or Apachae Hadoop.

## • Scrubbing The Data

After gaining the data and relevant information, the next instant thing to do is the cleaning and scrubbing of the data. This procedure is to clean and strain the data. If the information is unfiltered and inappropriate, then the effects of the inquiry and analysis will not make any sense.

During this procedure, the data is converted from one arrangement to another. It is recommended to combine everything into one consistent arrangement. For example, if you have data in different Excel files, then it is suggested to combine all the Excel files in to one excel file containing all the data. Scrubbing the data also includes the job of mining and substituting values. If it is found that there are lost data groups or the data appears to be non-values, a data expert substitutes the values accordingly. The data needs to be divided, combined, and extracted properly. This procedure is used for cleaning up the data, eliminating what is not required anymore, substituting what is lost, and regulating the format over which all the data is collected.

For doing the above-mentioned processes, a data expert will need a grasp of a good programming language for scrubbing the data. For the management of larger data groups, it is required to have skills in Hadoop and Spark.

- **Exploring The Data**

The third step is the examination of the extracted data. Typically, in a business or corporate environment, the managers just give a group of data to the experts, and they will study the data. The data scientists will figure out the corporate questions and alter the information into a data science query. To achieve this, an exploration of the data is essential. Data experts need to review the data and their characteristics. Different types of data require different actions. Examining important variables frequently is done with the help of the association.

For the above-mentioned task, a data scientist needs to have information and abilities in inferential data and information visualization.

## ● Modeling The Data

This is the 4th stage in the data science process, and it is considered the most important stage in the entire data science project lifecycle. To get to this stage, the cleaning of data and exploration of data are extremely important as those two phases lead to making useful and meaningful models. Firstly, decrease the dimensionality of your information group. All the values are not vital to forecasting the model. Just consider the applicable values that give an estimate of the results. Many tasks can be performed using modeling. Regular expressions and predictions are used for predicting future values. The evaluation total is carried out after the modeling process.

For the above tasks, both supervised and unsupervised algorithms are required.

## ● Understanding Of The Data

This is the final step of the entire data science process. This step is the most crucial in the entire process. The prognostic control of a model is present in its skill to generalize. A data scientist will describe a model based on the model's capacity to simplify hidden forthcoming data. Understandable data means the appearance of data to a non-technical person. This final step gives the results to deliver a solution to the business questions that were asked when the project was first started. In this process, the actionable understandings are offered through the data science process. Actionable understandings are key outcomes that demonstrate how data science can deal with projecting analytics and prescriptive investigations. Data experts need to envision the conclusions and keep them focused in correspondence with the corporate questions. It is vital to present the results properly. The results should be useful to the business.

For the tasks mentioned above, data scientists need to have a robust business area understanding to show the results in such a way that it provides answers to the business questions.

The above mentioned 5 steps demonstrate the life cycle of a data science project. Every data scientist follows these 5 steps to answer questions related to the field of data science.

CHAPTER 7:

# Capture, Process, Visualize, Analyze, Apply and Revert

I f we wanted to map how a factory works, we'd probably start with a description of the manufacturing process, but not necessarily focus on descriptions of particular jobs or machines placed along the production line. Instead, we'd start with a simple angle: this is what starts at the front end, and here are the basic steps taken to produce so-and-so output at the back end. Afterward, there'd be any amount of detailed descriptions of what those steps might be, and the technologies used to accomplish them.

So, let's approach a big data project in the same way. Any big data project involves seven core activities.

Some of these can be accomplished independently of others, in other words, you don't have to do all seven activities every time you want to execute a project, but all seven activities are reflected in, or used by, any project you might take on.

# Capture

As you might guess, it is the act of collecting information, or data. It's the starting point for any project because data is a raw resource. And we mean raw because data can come in many formats. The important line that helps us define data separates "structured" from "unstructured" data...

Structured data is anything that's been entered into an established form or process for capturing it; think of the fields you've been asked to fill out when ordering something from an online store, or employee records entered into a database intended to track whatever qualities your company wants to remember. It's also data that's been collected automatically, such as repeat visits to a website from a particular shopper, or a smart streetlamp that captures the volume of traffic that passes by.

This data can be easily searched by an algorithm, which is simply a kind of program that solves a problem through a specific set of operations. So, you can, quite literally, tell it where to look and what to compare, whether you're interested in numbers or words. It's the 'relational capacity' of structured data — the ability to make "apples to apples" comparisons — that makes it useful. The chances are that your company possesses lots of this data, especially as it relates to your customers- Which is why big data is used so often by marketers.

Unstructured data is, quite simply, everything else. Emails are unstructured data, as are text messages. The information contained in a video or audio recording is unstructured (and, so far, actually impossible for consumers to search). In fact, the entire World Wide Web consists of unstructured data, which is what Google helps overcome by using crawlers and other tools to capture information that can be used to create somewhat similar, and therefore comparable descriptions of what wildly different websites contain. It's difficult for most companies to use unstructured data.

The easiest and most profitable big data solutions will likely rely on structured data, whether you already possess it, or design a project to capture it. The distinctions between structured and unstructured data shouldn't really impact the capture phase of a project. However, in that you don't really want to preclude information until you have a full view of what's available to you.

So, the capture phase usually involves feeding all sorts of data into something called "Data Lake," which is literally what the name implies. The non-technical aspect of the capture phase is having visibility into what you know about something. Not conclusions, but what information about a subject is available to you.

## Process

Which is where companies define what they want to look at, how they're going to do it, and all the while guided by a clear picture of why. When it comes to processing your data, you don't always need an exact idea of what you think the data will show you, but instead, a reason for why you want to look at X, Y, or Z. Your process could be guided by a declarative intention, such as: "I want to improve production scheduling, so I want to know what times during the day our suppliers make deliveries, and correlate that with the weather." Or you might just have a more general curiosity about impacts on deliveries and therefore include more data variables in your process.

Put simply, people tend to find what they're looking for, so the key to a successful process is to know what data you want to look at more than forcing the outcome you think you want to find. Successful data science relies on posing good questions more than dictating exactly what will be the best or most important sources for answers.

What matters is the "how" of your process, or what you want to compare, or relate. Think of John Snow and his decision to correlate outbreaks of cholera in London with the locations of water pumps; what drove that process was his assumption that there might be a connection, but he could have just as easily looked at incidences of the disease correlated with bakeries, or some other variables. He just happened to be looking to prove or disprove a very specific hypothesis, and it turned out that he was correct. The relative ease of today's computational power allows us to pose broader, and more numerous hypotheses.

## Visualize

As all of us can remember at least one instance of being presented with, say, a huge spreadsheet of information and asking ourselves, "what exactly am I looking at, or looking for?" A whole host of formats can be used for data visualization, and there is any number of software tools available to render them.

The important parameters of visualization are what data do you want to see, how do you want to express the relationships within and between them, and how much do you want to interact with it (and change the connections or other parameters to yield different insights). The answer to the "what data?" question should be reasonably obvious, since it's mainly determined by what information you chose to study in the process. How you express it can get really interesting and fun, since there are many ways to do it.

Numeric representation is the most obvious, and a few columns of numbers don't have to be mind-numbingly boring, especially if you've wisely used colors, highlighting, and so on. What's good about expressing output in numbers is that the format, often a spreadsheet, is easily shared. Charts are also sharable, and can be far more impactful. If your output is in words, you can use things like word clouds to communicate importance and relationships. Maps are also very commonly used in big data projects, because the location can play such an important role in understanding the behaviors of customers, suppliers, and other groups.

You will often see a few, or many of these outputs aggregated into dashboards, which are used by marketers to track aspects of customer behavior or, in growing numbers, various aspects of healthcare big data insights. Beyond these, with a little research and expertise there are some seriously interesting ways to visualize your output, such as using 3D rendering, which is sometimes used to simulate the interaction between multiple data points. The trick here is to ensure that your visualization matches the needs and tastes of the people who need to consume and use the data.

There's no "right" answer other than meeting that requirement, and enabling your users to literally see clearly the correlations that your data process reveals.

## Store

We're not going to spend a lot of time on the next destination on our roadmap — which is Store — because how and where your big data results are stored is something that an actual IT person needs to decide, and manage from there. This is not to downplay its importance at all – it's just that the technical qualities of that activity are handled by specialists, and rightly so. Dealing with consumer data means you must keep up-to-date with changes in legislation, as governmental bodies in Europe, the US and elsewhere are currently refining their attitudes towards privacy, security and transparency.

Keeping data secure is made that much more complex when it's constantly traveling between locations and the cloud obviously carries a whole host of potential risks. And it's not just for the benefit of all the people whose data you're handling, various "duty to notify laws" require you to inform users and partners of breaches, something that could trigger civil fines and litigation. Failure to notify might be a serious criminal offense. Also, your data and insights are valuable assets that a competitor might want to access, or a hacker might want to kidnap and hold for ransom via encryption. Or simply destroy for the sheer sake of it. Normal enterprise IT security protocols need to be revisited in such cases, especially since it's likely a big data project will span multiple touchpoints.

As a client or user of big data, your security protections should be as important to you as the insights your data might yield. This includes developing usage rules for who can access the information, from where, and what rights they possess to change or download the data. And most importantly, always follow digital security best practice to keep risk to a minimum.

## Analyze and Apply

And it's where things really get going. Analysis means reaching conclusions, or newer hypotheses, based on the data you've visualized. A common analytic tool is called "segmentation," which simply means putting like evidenced data into the same segment, bucket, or group.

Analysis of your data might tell you that certain customers buy at certain times each day, but only from certain locations. It might reveal that employees whose initial resumes were longer tend to stay employed for fewer months than those with shorter ones, or that lights in offices that are turned off fewer than 3 times a day last longer than those that are turned off more often. The number of analytic outcomes is truly infinite; so what you want to do in this step is draw the conclusions that are most overt, supported by the most data points, and create in your mind (and not only on a computer screen) a group of people, or events, that are similar. Not surprisingly, segmentation has proven uses in marketing, where you can collect similar customers into a group or class that's identified by shared attributes, and then create communications tailored for them. But it's just as easily applied to devices or event. Any set of variables from which patterns might emerge. Studies of prices, for instance, can be modeled in this way. So can the probability of business outcomes, so imagine analyzing how sales or partnership deals are completed.

Usually, the Analyze stage means identifying a strong correlation between variables; your data cannot prove causation, in and of itself, but it can make it 'all but certain,' at least enough so that you can make business decisions based on it. It's worth stressing that your big data analysis will not tell you why things happen, or are connected, but only that they seem to be, perhaps consistently and inescapably. That's why the analysis step is as much about your business strategy processes as anything else; big data won't tell you what to do, but it will show you the potential for doing things.

It's also when you revisit the hypotheses or assumptions that you formulated at the beginning of the project, and ask yourself if the visualized findings prove or disprove them. It's also where you need to keep your mind open to discovering unexpected patterns, or the lack of ones you otherwise assumed existed, and brainstorm what that might mean.

CHAPTER 8:

# Benefits of Big Data

## Creating a Dialogue with Consumers

C onsumers in today's age are extremely tough nuts to crack. They don't easily make purchases and they like making informed decisions. Before making a purchase, they often like to look around for other options or browse through social media. They like being treated as unique, and then they expect to be thanked for making that purchase.

Big data will help you in profiling all such vocal and fickle consumers in a manner that can be thought of as a real-time conversation in this digital world. Don't think of this as a luxury. If they aren't treated the way they think they should be, then they will move to another source to make purchases without a second thought. For instance, when a customer enters a bank, then Big Data tools and platforms will allow the worker or clerk to check the customer's online profile and then learn about the relevant services or products that might interest the consumer.

Therefore, the consumer can also be made aware of the same, when looking for a reliable purchase or service. Big data will also help you in uniting the two distinct spheres of shopping in both the digital sense and the physical one. For instance, a retailer can offer a discount on a mobile carrier, based on the need of a consumer that was expressed on social media.

## Redeveloping Your Products

Big data can also help you in understanding the manner in which others perceive your products. This will let you make any changes to your product line or marketing techniques to meet current trends. Analyzing unstructured data present on social media will allow you to understand the opinions of your customers and segregate them into different geographical locations or identify them from different demographic classifications.

Big data will also let you test different variations of several computer aided programs that will help you in checking and keeping track of all the minor changes like the effects of cost, lead times and also the performance of a product on the market. You can also adapt your production process according to the needs of the public.

## Performing Risk Analysis

The success of your business depends on the way in which you handle your business dealings. However, there are several other social and economic factors that can affect your performance as well.

Predictive analytics that makes use of big data will allow you to scan and then even analyze reports mentioned in newspapers and various other social media feeds. This will allow you to stay on top of the latest developments that are taking place in your respective field. This also allows you to perform various "health" tests that will help you in identifying if any of your customers or suppliers are at risk of defaulting any of their payments or orders.

## Safekeeping of your Data

You will be able to take a look at the performance of your whole company by making use of different analytical tools. This will allow you to identify if there are any internal threats. By mapping out the data landscape, you will be able to find if any sensitive information isn't protected in the manner in which it should have been. If it isn't, then you can make sure that you are storing it in an appropriate manner. With data analytics, if you notice that any credit card information hasn't been stored properly, then the same can be flagged to prevent any damage and also to avoid this happening in the future.

## Creation of New Streams of Revenue

The various insights that you can gather from analyzing the market and its various consumers aren't just valuable to you alone. You can even sell them as trend data to any other bigger players in the market that are operating in the same segment.

This will help you in creating an entirely different stream of revenue for yourself. An impressive real-life example would be the popular song identification application, Shazam. Shazam helps the record labels and music houses to identify where the different subcultures in music are coming from by monitoring the service it provides. This includes the tracking of the data regarding the location that the mobile applications provide easily. This will enable the record labels to launch new artists who would suit the preferences of the audience or remarket the existing ones again. The criteria for using this app is that you want to know what a certain music track is, and of course, that means you, as a customer, are showing an interest in that music. That's useful information for record companies.

## Customizing your Website

Big data will allow you to customize and personalize the content, feel and look of your website. You can do so in real-time so that it can suit the needs of the different consumers who are entering it depending upon their sex, nationality or any other factor that leads them to your website. The best example of this would be the customized list of recommendations that Amazon provides. It does so by making use of a filtering technique that makes use of real-time data, and also the purchase history for suggesting other products. This is similar to the "People you may know" feature that is provided by LinkedIn and other various networking sites. This approach does work, and the data provided by

Amazon shows that this has helped them in increasing their revenue by 20%.

## Reducing the Cost of Maintenance

Usually, factories tend to have an estimate about the life span of a certain type of equipment and know how long it will last. As a result, they end up replacing such equipment within that assumed span of time, even if the machinery has got a few more years of useful life. Tools that analyze big data will be able to do away with such practices that aren't practical or even economical. These tools have got access to massive amounts of data and they can spot discrepancies quickly. They use this to estimate the average lifespan of the device. As a result, the business will be able to make use of a replacement strategy that has a greater utility and has less downtime. Faulty equipment can be tracked more easily.

## Tailor-made Healthcare Plans

In the world that we are living in, personalization is the mantra. Healthcare is still one sector where the trend of personalization still hasn't caught up. When someone has been diagnosed with cancer, they will have to undergo therapy. If that proves to be ineffective, they will have to go to another doctor and so on. Wouldn't it be helpful if the cancer patient could receive medication that is tailor made to suit his genes? This will not only allow for the reduction of costs, but it will also help in achieving better results. Human genome mapping isn't a concept that's far away in the future, due to the leaps in medicine and technology. The kind of potential of big data in the healthcare system is vast.

## Extensive Insights

If a business user wanted to analyze huge amounts of data, then it would be quite normal for the IT department to help them since they probably don't possess the technical skills for doing that. However, by the time they receive such information, it may have ceased to be of any use for them. Big data tools help in simplifying the work of the technical team by laying down the groundwork. Then they will simply have to develop algorithms that will help them in analyzing the data that is already available.

Every business tries to enhance the customer satisfaction that it can provide to improve their profitability. According to the needs of the company, the target markets of different businesses and industries as a whole keep on changing. The societal standards, needs and changing trends change the target audience as well. Being aware of this, it is quintessential to pull yourself ahead of all your completion through innovation and better services that will help in attracting and retaining customers.

Before business analytics has reached the stage it is at today, people in business had to make use of analytical models that were error-ridden. This potentially damaged their plans. Since it wasn't possible to extract and analyze data in a systematic manner, the earlier versions of analytics didn't prove to be of much use. The traditional teams that were involved in research and analytics had to spend long hours trying to gather information from all their customers. Statistical analysis helps in decision-making, and it requires the collection of data. Decision-making is a highly important process, and it shouldn't be overlooked at any cost. Even a minor error can damage the business. How exactly does analytics work and what are the benefits of making use of analytics in business? Let us take a look at the various advantages of making use of analytics in business.

## Measuring Performance

Every business has a mission statement of its own. The mission statement represents the goals of the business and the value they are offering to their consumers. It could include their marketing plan or any other goal that they would want to achieve. Making use of the mission statement as a guideline, most businesses tend to either promote from within in an attempt to retain their employees. This is a helpful manner in which the success of the company can be judged, but it wouldn't be prudent to leave the business depending on old established ideals.

Values must be capable of being quantified and they should be expressed tangibly to generate profits for the business. Quantifying the values of the business will help in improving its analytical process since it will help in defining the goal of the business. When such values can be quantified, then the same can be conveyed to the employees to get a clearer view of what their performance should be like. The more informed the employees are, the better their products will be. Fresh blood also helps with the generation of new ideas.

## Better Decision-Making

Being able to access important data will give your business the power to make better decisions. Not only will it provide you with viable information, but it will also help you in making effective and efficient decisions. Companies can also maximize the applicability of these analytics for sharing the same information with as many employees as possible. A group will be able to analyze the data better, and you will be able to make decisions that are more objective if the opinions of different people are being taken into account.

## Provides Clearer Insights

The recent variations of analytics that have been developed give importance to the manner in which the data is being presented to the analytics team or department. Making use of detailed charts and graphs for better decision-making is a good idea. Visual representation not only makes it easier to grasp the gist of the analysis but also to understand it easily. With the visualization of data analytics, all the numbers and figures are simply presented concisely through appealing and organized charts and graphs. This helps people who are not so technical to understand.

CHAPTER 9:

# The Future of Data Science and Big Data

## The Future of Big Data

We are amid a seismic shift in the Data Science world. This realization is beginning to manifest itself in the marketplace, with the newer analytics tools focusing more on deriving insight from data than running reports and dashboards. Which is of course, the correct way to look at this problem or any problem—focus on the end goal, don't focus on the "how": keep your eye on the prize.

However, the tools available today are primarily old-school business intelligence tools that are being retrofitted as fast as possible to try to ride this wave. Whether or not they will actually succeed or a new generation of tools will need to emerge is still an open question.

With that in mind here are 5 developmental directions to watch:

# Your Data Will Tell You What Is Interesting

Current Business Intelligence does exactly the opposite: you tell your tool what you're interested in. The coming generation will tell you what's interesting.

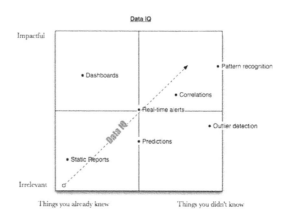

Generating these types of insights will become much easier in the coming years and personalization will have a lot to do with this. Think about how revolutionary Pandora was for music when you first tried it—it actually learns what you find interesting! This is the direction analytics is heading.

The systems themselves will also get better at automatic learning and pattern recognition, about what you want to see. This will enable them to spot outliers, trend changes, and other interesting data that. Today must be spotted by a human being.

## Wild Visualizations

Charts and graphs have been around for a long time. And there's a reason for that: they're good at conveying meaning in an easy-to-grasp way.

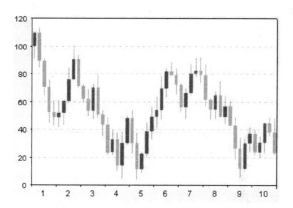

But again, they were developed as a way to understand much smaller amounts of data than we're looking at now. New ways of looking at data—and especially interacting with it—are being developed. Right now, we're seeing the first wave of this, where designers are trying things out and some work, some don't. Things like infographics, interactive Web pages, and some of the newer intelligence tools are examples of trying new ways of looking at data.

We expect to see this trend accelerate. And as the field becomes more popular and more vital to the world economy, the brains and time spent on this problem will lead to breakthroughs in new ways to look at and understand data.

## Self-Service Intelligence

The ability to use analytics will no longer be a specialized skill, and we already see the beginnings of this with Data Discovery tools. It will be a common and everyday thing for executives on down the line to use as part of their daily and hourly workflow. We've seen how this is playing out through IBM's Watson and it will be especially pervasive in the knowledge industry.

This is slightly counterintuitive because the amount of data being used is growing by the day, and yet the tools will be simpler? Yes, that's right.

As the amount of data increases, it is forcing a complete reevaluation of what intelligence tools need to be. The complex user interfaces with miles of toolbars and byzantine menu systems are no longer adequate— they were built for a world with much fewer data.

Which brings us to the new types of interfaces that are needed:

## Natural and Intuitive Interaction with Data

Business intelligence is one of the last bastions of enterprise-y software simply because of its complexity. You know you're using business intelligence software if half the screen is taken by menus and a passerby would have no idea what you're looking at.

Natural interfaces such as touch, voice, and gestures abstract away the complexity. The more functionality you can make intuitive the more productive a user can be, because they won't have to learn how to use it. When you can literally ask the question "what demographic should I focus on to increase sales?" You can find valuable information without training or expert help.

Apple did the world a great service by training people to use touch and coming up with intuitive—and, now, universally accepted—touch gestures. Apple's Siri is important because it is training people to use voice. Microsoft's Kinect is important because it's training people to use body gestures. All of these modes of input combined create an interactive environment that lets you play with your data—explore it and interact with it.

You will think with your eyes and follow your nose to the data you're looking for, even if you're not sure of the right question to ask.

Data will be fun.

## Collaborative

A few years ago, you couldn't escape "collaboration" as a buzzword. The idea was that by enabling people to work together, you freed them to pool their creative and mental resources. Hopefully, of course, resulting in a synergistic explosion of ideas and good decisions.

The collaboration was, in a sense, a way to deal with a lot of information—Big Data—before Big Data got really Big. Crowd-sourced report hunting, basically. Unfortunately the amount of data that needs to be evaluated is simply too big even for large numbers of people to efficiently looking at.

The new types of interfaces (as explained above) will alleviate that problem. But there was a core value in the collaboration that doesn't go away just because it's no longer "the new black". Two heads are still better than one, if they're in the right place at the right time.

When tools allow people to use intuitive interfaces to not only explore their data and discover from it but also to allow more than one person to do this at the same time, the results will be nothing short of magical. Imagine being able to look at data in interesting ways, exploring it and sharing what you're looking at in real-time with colleagues from around the world. Igniting conversations. Enabling people to work on the same thing but giving them the freedom to explore independently gives you the best of both worlds.

## But When?

Most of these changes will happen within the next 3 to 5 years. Some of them are happening already. But all signs point to a type of inevitability for them—they are at the intersection of two or larger trends driving our society towards a new type of information consumption. One that's very different from what you think of today.

**CHAPTER 10:**

# Big Data Analysis Applications

T here are already so many ways that this data analysis is going to be used, and when we can put it all together, we are going to see some amazing results in the process. Places like the financial world, security, marketing, advertising, and healthcare are all going to benefit from this data analysis, and as more time goes on, it is likely that we will see more of these applications as well. Some of the ways that we are able to work with data analysis and get the best results from it include:

## Security

There are several cities throughout the world that are working on predictive analysis so that they can predict the areas of the town where there is more likely to be a big surge for the crime that is there. This is done with the help of some data from the past and even data on the geography of the area.

This is actually something that a few cities in America have been able to use, including Chicago. Although we can imagine that it is impossible to use this to catch every crime that is out there, the data that is available from using this is going to make it easier for police officers to be present in the right areas at the right times to help reduce the rates of crime in some of those areas. And in the future, you will find that when we use data analysis in this kind of manner in the big cities have helped to make these cities and these areas a lot safer, and the risks would not have to put their lives at risk as much as before.

## Transportation

The world of transportation is able to work with data analysis, as well. A few years ago, when plans were being made at the London Olympics, there was a need during this event to handle more than 18 million journeys that were made by fans into the city of London. Moreover, it was something that we were able to sort out well.

How was this feat achieved for all of these people? The train operators and the TFL operators worked with data analytics to make sure that all those journeys went as smoothly as possible. These groups were able to go through and input data from the events that happened around that time and then used this as a way to forecast how many people would travel to it. This plan went so well that all of the spectators and the athletes could be moved to and from the right places promptly the whole event.

# Risk and Fraud Detection

This was one of the original uses of data analysis and was often used in the field of finance. There are many organizations that had a bad experience with debt, and they were ready to make some changes to this. Because they had a hold on the data that was collected each time that the customer came in for a loan, they were able to work with this process in order to not lose as much money in the process.

This allowed the banks and other financial institutions to dive and conquer some of the data from the profiles they could use from those customers. When the bank or financial institution is able to utilize their customers they are working with, the costs that had come up recently, and some of the other information that is important for these tools, they will make some better decisions about who to loan out money to, reducing their risks overall. This helps them to offer better rates to their customers.

In addition to helping these financial institutions make sure that they can hand out loans to customers who are more likely to pay them back, you will find that this can be used in order to help cut down on the risks of fraud as well. This can cost the bank billions of dollars at year and can be expensive to work with. When the bank can use all of the data that they have for helping discover transactions that are fraudulent and making it easier for their customers to keep money in their account, and make sure that the bank is not going to lose money in the process as well.

## Logistics of Deliveries

There are no limitations when it comes to what we are able to do with our data analysis, and we will find that it works well when it comes to logistics and deliveries. There are several companies that focus on logistics, which will work with this data analysis, including UPS, FedEx, and DHL. They will use data in order to improve how efficient their operations are all about.

From applications of analytics of the data, it is possible for these companies who use it to find the best and most efficient routes to use when shipping items, the ones that will ensure the items will be delivered on time, and so much more. This helps the item to get things through in no time, and keeps costs down to a minimum as well. Along with this, the information that the companies are able to gather through their GPS can give them more opportunities in the future to use data science and data analytics.

## Customer Interactions

Many businesses are going to work with the applications of data analytics in order to have better interactions with their customers. Companies can do a lot about their customers, often with some customer surveys. For example, many insurance companies are going to use this by sending out customer surveys after they interact with their handler. The insurance company is then able to use which of their services are good, that the customers like, and which ones they would like to work on to see some improvements.

There are many demographics that a business is able to work with and it is possible that these are going to need many diverse methods of communication, including email, phone, websites, and in-person interactions. Taking some of the analysis that they can get with the demographics of their customers and the feedback that comes in, it will ensure that these insurance companies can offer the right products to these customers, and it depends one hundred percent on the proven insights and customer behavior as well.

## City Planning

Web traffic and marketing are actually the things that are being used instead of the creation of buildings and spaces. This is going to cause many of the issues that are going to come up when we talk about the power over our data is because there are some influences over building zoning and creating new things along the way in the city.

Models that have been built well are going to help maximize the accessibility of specific services and areas while ensuring that there is not the risk of overloading significant elements of the infrastructure in the city at the same time. This helps to make sure there is a level of efficiency as everyone, as much as possible, is able to get what they want without doing too much to the city and causing harm in that manner.

We will usually see buildings that are not put in the right spots or businesses that are moved where they do not belong. How often have you seen a building that was on a spot that looked like it was suitable and good for the need, but which had a lot of negative impact on other places around it? This is because these potential issues were not part of the consideration during the planning period. Applications of data analytics, and some modeling, helps us to make things easier because we will know what would happen if we put that building or another item on that spot that you want to choose.

## Healthcare

The healthcare industry has been able to see many benefits from data analysis. There are many methods, but we are going to look at one of the main challenges that hospitals are going to face. Moreover, this is that they need to cope with cost pressures when they want to treat as many patients as possible while still getting high-quality care to the patients. This makes the doctors and other staff fall behind in some of their work on occasion, and it is hard to keep up with the demand.

You will find that the data we can use here has risen so much, and it allows the hospital to optimize and then track the treatment of their patient. It is also a good way to track the patient flow and how the different equipment in the hospital is being used. In fact, this is so powerful that it is estimated that using this data analytics could provide a 1 percent efficiency gain, and could result in more than $63 billion in worldwide healthcare services. Think of what that could mean to you and those around you.

Doctors are going to work with data analysis in order to provide them with a way to help their patients a bit more. They can use this to make some diagnoses and understand what is going on with their patients in a timely and more efficient manner. This can allow doctors to provide their customers with a better experience and better care while ensuring that they can keep up with everything they need to do.

## Travel

Data analytics and some of their applications are a good way to help optimize the buying experience for a traveler. This can be true through a variety of options, including data analysis of mobile sources, websites, or social media. The reason for this is because the desires and the preferences of the customer can be obtained from all of these sources, which makes companies start to sell out their products thanks to the correlation of all the recent browsing on the site and any of the currency sells to help purchase conversions. They are able to utilize all of this to offer some customized packages and offers. The applications of data analytics can also help to deliver some personalized travel recommendations, and it often depends on the outcome that the company is able to get from their data on social media.

## Digital Advertising

Outside of just using it to help with some searching another, there is another area where we are able to see data analytics happen regularly, and this is digital advertisements. From some of the banners that are found on several websites to the digital billboards that you may be used to seeing in some of the bigger and larger cities, but all of these will be controlled thanks to the algorithms of our data along the way.

This is a good reason why digital advertisements are more likely to get a higher CTR than the conventional methods that advertisers used to rely on a lot more. The targets are going to work more on the past behaviors of the users, and this can make for some good predictions in the future.

**CHAPTER 11:**

# Making It Big with Big Data

This is going to be a term that is used in order to describe the large volume of data, which can be either unstructured or structured or both, that is going to come to a business on a daily basis. While most of the time, we are talking about a large amount of data, this isn't the important part when we talk about this. Instead, the part that is the most important here is how the company is able to take that data and use it. Big data can be analyzed so that the company can learn valuable insights that will lead them to the best business moves and much better decisions than before.

When it comes to big data, there are a lot of different parts that come together to work with this term. While this term, in particular, is still pretty new, the act of being able to gather and store a lot of information to be used in the analysis has been around for years. Companies have always been in the market to take as much information as they can and use it to help them out. This information, if they are able to sort through it the proper way, and find the right insights, can give them a competitive edge in the world and will make it easier for them to get ahead while serving their customers.

With this in mind, there are a few definitions out there for what big data is all about and how it works. There are going to be three main Vs that we can use to help us get a better understanding of this big data, and how we are able to use it for our needs.

The first V here is Volume. With this one, a company is going to take some time to collect their data, often from a wide variety of sources. Relying on data from just one source may seem like it is easier, but it is not the best for building sound business decisions. There are many different ways that this information can be gathered, including from the transactions of the business, social media, surveys, and more. In the past, though, being able to store this information, and even getting through it, would have been a problem. But now there are a lot of different technologies and platforms that can handle this information and helps the company to gather as much information as they would like, without worrying about where they should store it.

The second V we need to focus on is the Velocity. The data that a company is going to get is able to stream in at a very fast speed, something that we haven't seen in the past, and we need to make sure that this data is being dealt with, not sometime in the future, in within a timelier manner. Things like sensors and RFID tags are going to help us to get through this information and make it work with us, going at near real-time in the process.

And the third V is Variety. The best kind of data is the kind that has a lot of variety. This is going to ensure that the business is getting the information that it needs, without getting stuck on one tangent along the way. The data that the company uses can come in many different formats. This could include financial transactions, data from the stock tickers, audio, video, emails, text documents that are not structured, structured data, and even some numeric data that we are able to find in some of the traditional databases.

While those three components can tell us a lot about big data and the information that we are going to be able to get out of it, there are also two other dimensions that we may want to look at as well to determine what big data is all about and how it is going to work. These two additional dimensions are going to include the complexity and the variability of the data that we are working with.

The first dimension that we are going to look at here is the variability. In addition to being able to increase both the varieties and the velocities of data, the flow of data can sometimes be very inconsistent, and it is going to come with some periodic peaks that can mess with the information. This is something that can show up often when we are talking about social media.

While these peaks are sometimes seen as a good thing because it means that our customers are there and providing us with more information for us to get better, these peaks, whether they are triggered seasonally, daily, and even by an event, can be hard for a company to learn how to manage. And when these peaks are happening with data that is not structured, the challenge is going to become even more pronounced.

And the final dimension that we are going to look at for this part is going to be the complexity. You can imagine that the data a company gets from its customers, services, and products are going to come from more than one source.

Now that we understand a bit more about how this is going to work, it is time to move on and explore some of the reasons why big data is so important.

The importance that we are going to find when it comes to big data is that it really doesn't revolve around the amount of data that you have. While it is true that most companies are going to have a ton of data, some companies that may have a little less can gain a competitive advantage because they are able to better use the data that is available for them. What is most important when we are talking with this is what you decide to do with the data that is presented to you.

It is possible for a company to take in data from any kind of source and then take some time to analyze it to find the answers that are needed. The answers that you are looking for will depend on what kind of business you are running, and what your own end goals and plans are. This data, when it is used in the proper manner, is able to help us reduce costs, reduce the amount of time it takes to get things done, can help us optimize the products and offerings that are there for the customers, and ensures that all the decisions that are made are smart decisions.

When you are able to take all of that data that a company has been collecting for some time, and then combine it together with some higher-powered analytics, there are going to be a few different tasks related to a business that you are able to do. Some of the tasks that are possible when you combine the data with the analytics include:

- Big data can be used in order to detect when there is some kind of behavior that is seen as fraudulent before it is able to affect your business and cause a mess.

- Big data is able to come in and recalculate the entire risk of your portfolio in just a few minutes.

- You can use big data to make the shopping experience for your customers more friendly. It is going to be useful at generating coupons at the point of sale based on the buying habits that are seen for your customers.

- Big data can be used to help determine some of the root causes of failures, defects, and issues in near real-time in the process.

There are many companies and industries that do not worry about using big data at all. They may be collecting data and looking through it on occasion, but they are worried that they are not able to use it in the right way, or that it will take too long. These companies are wasting their potential in many cases, and this data is just sitting there without being used the way that it should.

But almost all industries are going to use this big data in order to see the results that they need for being competitive and getting ahead in the market. Big data is going to be able to help organizations in almost any kind of industry that is out there. Let's take a look at some of the industries that are going to use this big data, along with some of the ways that they actually use this data.

The first industry that has been able to benefit when they use big data is going to be banking. Think about all of the data and information that a bank, even a small local one, is going to work with all of the time. This turns into a large amount of information that comes in from a ton of different sources. And because of all this, many banks are looking for new and innovative methods to help them manage their customers.

These banks also have the added issue of trying to make sure that the satisfaction from their customers is high while minimizing their own risk and preventing fraud all at the same time. Add this into that, and there are often going to be regulations on a state and national level, and it is hard for a bank to be able to manage it all. With the help of the big data that they have, banks are able to help meet all of these different requirements in one.

Another place where big data is going to be important is education. Educators are often going to need to be armed with a lot of insight if they want to make an impact not only on their school system but on the curriculum they pick and on the students. When the educators, whether these are teachers or principals or someone else in the school, choose to analyze all of the big data they have, it becomes easier to do their job.

Depending on the way that the educator decides to use this big data, they will be better prepared to identify students who are at risk and may need more help. They can make sure that all students are going to make the right kind of progress, and they can even go through the implementation process to make sure there is a better system for support and for evaluating every educator in the school system.

The government is another area that could utilize big data to make things better. Think of the vast amounts of data that governments are able to gather from citizens about what they do and use on a regular basis. Even our utility companies will have this kind of data to determine how much to charge, where to add new utility services, and more.

**CHAPTER 12:**

# Big Data Management – Too Big to Succeed?

M any worthwhile projects have never gotten off the ground because they were too big. By that standard, Big Data has little chance of garnering support unless leadership is willing to say Big Insights are worth the time and resources.

The first step for making the case to move forward is to break down the project into the primary components:

Data Inventory: Identity all internal, and relevant external, data sources. Document the owners, and managers of the data the format (SQL; Oracle, etc.) size frequency of updates, types of unstructured data, Internet of Things data sources, and highlight all sensitive data.

Data Access: Identify access requirements to all structured and unstructured data from the data sources inventoried. Determine how frequently the data will be updated. Real-time may sound like the obvious answer, but reality may show real-time is in fact, either not necessary or is too expensive to implement.

Insight Reservoir: Identify the environment where you will store, analyze, and govern your insights, as well as from which you will distribute such. On-premise, cloud-based, or hybrid is a critical decision. The staffing implications of each choice should be uppermost in your mind. Another consideration is whether you will be gathering real-time data. This will impact your choices and your costs.

Data Quality: Your data will never be perfect, but achieving the highest possible quality of data will increase confidence in the results. Certain data sources will have lower quality. Consider having a quality score for each data source, which can be used as part of your algorithms to increase or decrease the weight of a data source or data element. An example is professional data sourced from social media. This data has a higher likelihood of being out-of-date, inaccurate, or incomplete.

Master Data Management: Understanding your data across sources is essential to success. Your prospects and donors are unlikely to have a common ID across data sources, so you will need to create a "Golden Record," which tells you all of the information relating to a record. A good practice is to determine which of your IDs will be the Master ID. As part of this process, you will also decide on the terminology and business rules, to be used as you bring the data together. One data source might use the word revenue while another uses income. Without a common language, the analysis will be confusing to insight users.

Data Governance: In a Big Data environment Data Governance has to be integrated into the technology, so activity can be monitored and reported.

Big Insights: Gather organizational questions, and evaluate them in a Big Data context. Are multiple data sources required? Is there relevant unstructured data? What are your current questions and answers? What are the gaps in the insight they are delivering? All of these questions must be continually asked to ensure current realities. And future needs, are taken into account.

Actionable Insights: Mapping insights to insight users, and then to their potential actions will dramatically increase utilization. Determine which insight actions can be fully automated; automated with some insight user supervision; or only delivered to insight users for action. All of this needs to be fully documented and may involve Service Level Agreements between IT and insight users. While this may seem like overkill, it will build confidence with users, and also manage expectations.

Return on Insight (ROi): The final step is to look at how the return on Big Data will be evaluated. For financial factors establish "pre-Big Data" benchmarks. Non-financial factors could include donor retention, alumni participation, donor satisfaction, and mission delivery metrics. Look at the questions you have been asking, and evaluate the quality of the answers as part of your ROi analysis.

The technology needed to accomplish the project will depend in large part on whether you decide to implement an on-premise; cloud-based; or hybrid solution. No matter which you select, the tools involved will fall into the following areas:

Data Connection, Ingestion, and Processing: Tools to securely connect to any type of data source, ingestion of the data into a Big Data environment; and processing of the data to create a schema for analysis.

Data Administration and Security: Tools to govern, secure, and administer the transformation of data into what is needed for the creation of actionable insights based on organization, and regulatory policies.

Data Integration: Tools for establishing relationships between datasets, including entity resolution, in order to provide a cross-organizational view of all data.

Data Quality Assurance: Tools to identify and address inaccurate, incomplete, duplicate, and erroneous data on an on-going basis.

Data Cataloging: A cross-organizational repository for all of the metadata relating to data assets. This includes all processes for integrating, securing, and governing those assets.

Master Data Management: Tools to provide a cross-organizational reference source to ensure the accuracy of data and the relevance of the insights provided.

Sensitive Data Masking: Tools to remove, protect, or obscure sensitive data, including personally identifiable information (PII) and demographically identifiable information, social security numbers, credit card numbers, health information, mission beneficiary information, and student records.

Data Security Monitoring: Tools to continually track and analyze security vulnerabilities, including points of access, user activity, and accessing sensitive data.

Cognitive Analytics: Tools to create algorithms and formulas based on the analysis of datasets. These tools need to go beyond traditional business intelligence tools, enabling such things as machine learning and cluster analytics.

Streaming Analytics: Tools to process data in real-time, or near real-time. The insights may be integrated with an alert system and/or incorporated into analysis with lower latency datasets.

Insight Reservoir: A platform to securely collect, store, manage, and analyze all your structured and unstructured data. If a data warehouse is utilized to store structured information for business intelligence and reporting, the data warehouse will become a source of data for the Insight Reservoir.

Now you have a better understanding of the key aspects of a Big Data project, and the tools you will need to be successful. Now let's tackle staffing. Depending on the size of your organization, you may have little or no internal capability to implement and manage a Big Data project. If you work within a large organization you may have some or even all of the skills currently on staff, but those colleagues may be overwhelmed with current obligations.

The following is a list of personnel you will need if you decide to fully implement and manage in-house:

- Project Manager

- System Administrator

- Network Administrator

- Database Administrator

- IT Security

- Business Intelligence Analyst

- Data Scientist

- Java Hadoop Developer

## Q&A Engineer

The cost of these positions will, of course, change based on where your organization is located, but also keep in mind there is fierce competition for people who have experience implementing Big Data. My recommendation, unless you have a strong IT team, is for you to outsource as much of the technical aspects as possible while keeping data science capabilities in-house as well as Data Governance management. Even if you are confident in your IT capabilities, still look at bringing in help for implementation to ensure it is done right, and minimizes the disruption of your current operations.

Transitioning your prospect research team into insight analysts is another important step in becoming an insight-driven organization.

You have looked at the elements of the project; the technology you will need, and the staffing. Now it is time to take an honest look at your organization's readiness to embrace Big Data.

There are many assessment tools. One I like to be by Transforming Data with Intelligence (TDWI), a division of 1105 Media, Inc. They offer an online assessment you can take at no cost. It breaks down organizational maturity into five levels:

1.  NASCENT: Little or no understanding among the leadership about what Big Data is or what it could do for the organization. May have implemented a data warehouse and done basic business intelligence around key performance indicators.

2.  PRE-ADOPTION: Some technology may have been purchased or rented, such as Hadoop, to create a test environment. At this stage, the project is often driven at the departmental level.

3.  EARLY ADOPTION: Proofs-of-concept (POC) dominate this stage. A couple may have made it to production where insights are being acted on. A reason there can be a chasm between this stage and the next is the time it may take to realize ROI. I ran into this issue with wealth screening. While organizations were identifying new prospects, they still had to go through the solicitation cycle. This caused an 18-36 month delay between receiving the data and realizing the benefit. The good news is once the gifts started rolling in, the adoption of wealth screening increased dramatically. I believe the same thing will happen with Big Data.

The Chasm - The success of the early adoption stage will trigger a series of events, which will delay full implementation across the organization. These include the need for a budget to support additional staffing and technology acquisition; political barriers, including data ownership, will need to be handled; a data governance structure will need to be created;

security will need to be upgraded; and other departments who may not have been part of the POC will need to be brought into the mix.

4.   CORPORATE ADOPTION: This is the major phase of Big Data adoption as the organization makes it an integral part of its operations. A cross-section of users will be using insights, and the organizational structure to support long-term adoption has been put in place. Another hallmark of this stage is changes in how decisions are made through using the insights now available.

5.   MATURE/VISIONARY: Very few companies, much fewer NGOs, have attained this stage. Those that have are executing Big Data projects on an on-going basis and are budgeted and well-planned. Big Data has created an atmosphere of excitement and energy around the insights being derived and the potential for future insights. I see this stage as having moved from fearing the future to embracing the future.

It is interesting to note the chasm between early adoption and corporate adoption. This captures a reality of Big Data projects, which is they often begin on a small scale within a part of the organization, and then grow to a point where leadership green lights a proof-of-concept.

If the proof-of-concept (POC) takes longer than expected and/or does not produce measurable results, then into the chasm they go. The lesson is to carefully plan the POC, so the scope does not get out hand in terms of cost and time. Also, make sure the focus is on delivering an insight you know leadership cares about and the organization and staff can act on.

# Conclusion

T hank you for making it to the end. I'd like to conclude by talking a bit about the implications of the big data revolution we are experiencing. There are two main threads that fit into this discussion. The first is the possibility of massive job losses and upheaval of the economy as a result of these new technologies. The second thread involves privacy issues.

When we think about new technology, we tend to think in terms of gadgets. The first thing that might come to mind is your cell phone. Self-driving cars, spaceflight, and other technologies that you can hold in your hand or see also intrigue us.

For this reason, big data is an unusual development in the history of technology. It is largely unseen by the general public even though you are feeling its effects. Also, in the process of analyzing big data, there are analysts, statistical models, fast computer systems, along with a large computer storage systems and cloud computing. If people think about it at all, they would probably be focused on the computers themselves. However, it is the data on the hard drives and the software algorithms that analyze that data which is important.

When you consider all the technologies that have been developed in the last fifty years, many of them pale in significance compared to big data. For example, think of all the attention that has been lavished on cell phones. For all the wonder that a device like an iPhone provides, its impact on society at large won't be near the impact of big data and machine learning.

For example, a smartphone is unlikely to cause you to lose your job. However, big data in machine learning may do exactly that. Whether that matters to you, one thing we know for certain is that possibly millions of jobs will be eliminated over a very short time. It is too early to determine what the impact of this will be. In several instances in the past, new technologies have created far more jobs than they destroyed. In fact, that has always been the case ever since the Industrial Revolution started. We already talked about the example of the textile machines and the Luddites, but there are even more recent examples. Those under the age of forty probably are not aware of what life was like prior to the massive adoption of computer systems. In the 1970s and even into the 1980s, many businesses did spreadsheet work by hand. Secretaries were used to typing documents on typewriters.

At that time, spreadsheet programs and word processors we are rapidly gaining the market share as businesses adopted them. This scared many people at the time.

People imagined that the office would soon become free of paper and that the advent of spreadsheets and word processors would eliminate millions of jobs.

The same thing happened the more these technologies became used in more and more offices. Rather than eliminate jobs, the impact was to create millions of new jobs instead. This happens because productivity is massively increased with each introduction of new technology. Second, it frees people from trivial tasks they were devoting their time to before. A strange thing happens as these patterns develop. People find out that new must-do and must-have things become required in the new economy that springs out of the chaos.

That is likely to be the case this time as well. Although robotics will certainly eliminate many jobs, new jobs that you cannot even imagine right now will spring up in their place. Some people cite the rapid pace of transformation as a reason to be pessimistic about this. However, it should be noted that this will also cause an explosion in the pace of change, which brings about an entirely new business in place of the old jobs lost to robotics and artificial intelligence.

Another thing that happens during a transformation process like this is that the economy itself grows by a large amount, so even if you lost a certain number of jobs, the growth of the economy, which is benefiting from the new technologies, will more than offset the loss of those jobs. There will always be jobs for humans to perform, so people might be doing new things, but they will certainly have some things to do.

In fact, we already see this on a large-scale. When the internet became available to the general public and to businesses, it created many new jobs and job categories that did not exist before. This was also accompanied by changes generated by the existence of software programs such as Photoshop. Some new job categories that have proven very lucrative include web programmers, graphic designers, JavaScript programmers, and so forth. This has also happened with respect to mobile or smartphones. It is estimated that as a result of the iPhone, there are 1.5 million new jobs in the United States. These jobs are related to app development and include computer programming jobs, user interface design, graphic design, as well as millions of people who have started their own businesses centered on developing iPhone apps. The numbers are probably even larger when you consider Google's Android.

In addition, the video gaming industry is growing in leaps and bounds. Games continue to be developed for traditional devices like consoles, but many companies are only developing games for use on smartphones. This has created an entirely new set of job possibilities.

In my view, something similar will happen as artificial intelligence, big data, and machine learning continue to weave their way throughout our society.

Regarding the privacy issue, privacy and ethical concerns are certainly important. However, it is my opinion that big data has already won the day and won't go away anytime soon. In fact, the importance of big data will increase in the coming years, and its commercial impact is too large for companies to ignore. Not only does selling data provide a lucrative way to generate income, but big data also increases the power of marketing and advertising as well as customer service for large corporations. The benefits of this are just way too large, and no matter what politicians do, I don't believe they can stop this process.

With that in mind, we must consider protecting our own data, becoming more aware of the terms of service and privacy rules, and being more concerned about security. One factor that has made data sharing controversial is a simple fact people do not pay attention to. It is painful, but you must take the time to read software company documents regarding privacy. If Congress does anything, it might be helpful if they would require companies to present clear and easy-to-understand information related to these issues that could be read quickly by customers. Think about what happens nine times out of ten when people open a website or app and are faced with terms of service or privacy agreements. Most people are far too impatient to deal with this, and the legalese of these documents simply gives them a headache. So they quickly dismiss the document by agreeing to it.

Politicians are probably mistaken if they believe they will solve this problem by breaking up the big tech companies. Big data will still be there, and it will be worth more than ever if that happens. In my opinion, it is probably better to have a few powerful companies managing and controlling a large fraction of the data. In any case, if they break up these companies, the problem will just shift around rather than go away. It might also be harder for governments to regulate, which would defeat their purpose. I tend to take a libertarian view as long as there is not abuse, so in my opinion, the company should not be broken up. However, there should be some simple regulations put in place to ensure that people can protect their privacy. Data sharing should be allowed, but no one should be able to identify specific individuals in that data.

I hope you have learned something!